A Note to Parents

DK READERS is a compelling program for beginning readers, designed in conjunction with leading literacy experts, including Dr. Linda Gambrell, Director of the Eugene T. Moore School of Education at Clemson University. Dr. Gambrell has served on the Board of Directors of the International Reading Association and as President of the National Reading Conference.

Beautiful illustrations and superb full-color photographs combine with engaging, easy-to-read stories to offer a fresh approach to each subject in the series. Each DK READER is guaranteed to capture a child's interest while developing his or her reading skills, general knowledge, and love of reading.

The five levels of DK READERS are aimed at different reading abilities, enabling you to choose the books that are exactly right for your child:

Pre-level 1: Learning to read
Level 1: Beginning to read
Level 2: Beginning to read alone
Level 3: Reading alone
Level 4: Proficient readers

The "normal" age at which a child begins to read can be anywhere from three to eight years old, so these levels are only a general guideline.

No matter which level you select, you can be sure that you are helping your child learn to read, then read to learn!

DK

LONDON, NEW YORK, MUNICH,
MELBOURNE, AND DELHI

Series Editor Deborah Lock
Designer Sadie Thomas
U.S. Editor Elizabeth Hester
Production Alison Lenane
DTP Designer Almudena Díaz
and Pilar Morales
Jacket Designer Simon Oon

Reading Consultant
Linda Gambrell, Ph.D.

First American Edition, 2004
20 19 18 17
022-AD167-Oct/04
Published in the United States by DK Publishing, Inc.
345 Hudson Street, New York, New York 10014

Published in Great Britain by Dorling Kindersley Limited

Library of Congress Cataloging-in-Publication Data
Farm animals.-- 1st American ed.
    p. cm. -- (DK readers, pre-level 1)
    ISBN-13: 978-0-7566-0536-0 (pbk.).
    1. Livestock--Juvenile literature. I. Dorling Kindersley readers. Pre-level
1, Learning to read.
    SF75.5.F367 2004
    636--dc22   6928
                                                    2004007457

Color reproduction by Colourscan, Singapore
Printed and bound in the US by Lake Book Manufacturing, Inc.

The publisher would like to thank the following for their kind
permission to reproduce their photographs:
a=above; c=center; b=below; l=left; r=right t=top;

www.agripicture.com: Peter Dean 22–23. **Alamy Images:** Bildagentur
Geduldig/archivberlin Fotoagentur GmbH 18-19; Jack Sullivan 26-27.
Ardea.com: John Daniels 10-11. **Corbis:** Darrell Gulin 8-9; Kit Houghton
24-25; Randy M. Ury 4-5. **DK Picture Library:** Barleylands Farm Museum
and Animal Centre 6, 8–9, 16; Philip Dowell 12, 14, 15, 18; Jerry Young
15; Tracy Morgan 15; Odds Farm Park 19; Barrie Watts 20, 21.
Getty Images: Pal Hermansen 20t; Hans Reinhard 11t. **Holt Studios
International:** 15t. **Oxford Scientific Films:** Mark Hamblin 14-15;
Konrad Wothe 12t.

All other images © Dorling Kindersley
For further information see: www.dkimages.com

Discover more at
www.dk.com

DK READERS

LEARNING
pre-level
1
TO READ

Farm
Animals

DK Publishing, Inc.

Come and meet
my friends
on the farm.

farmhouse

barn

feathers

chickens

Here is the chicken
with her little chicks.

chick

Here is the turkey coming to meet you.

beak

  turkeys

feathers

Here is the pig.
Here are three
pink piglets.

piglet

 pigs

ear

Here are the cows looking at you.

hoof

COWS

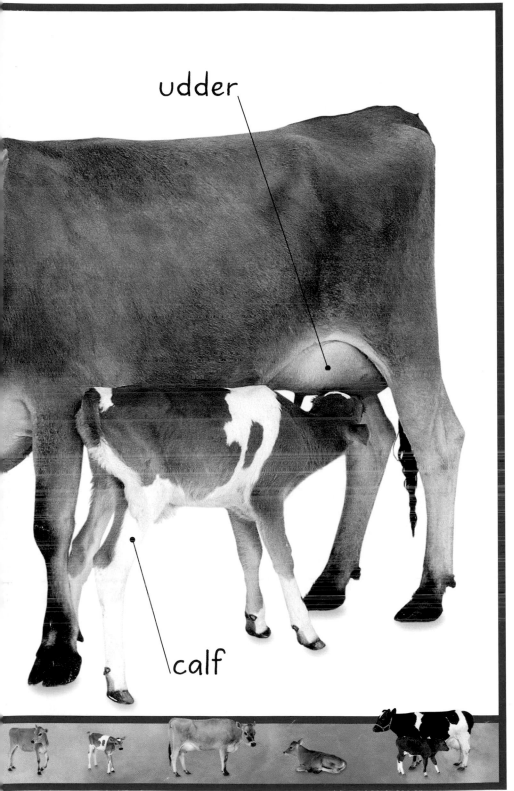

udder

calf

13

Here is the dog.
Here are three
sleepy puppies.

nose

puppy

dogs

Here are the sheep with a little lamb.

lamb

sheep

wool

ear

nose

goats

Here is the goat lying down with her kid.

kid

Here are the ducks
with their
fluffy ducklings.

 ducks

20

beak

duckling

Here are
the white geese
looking all around.

 geese

eye

neck

Here is the horse
running with her foal.

foal

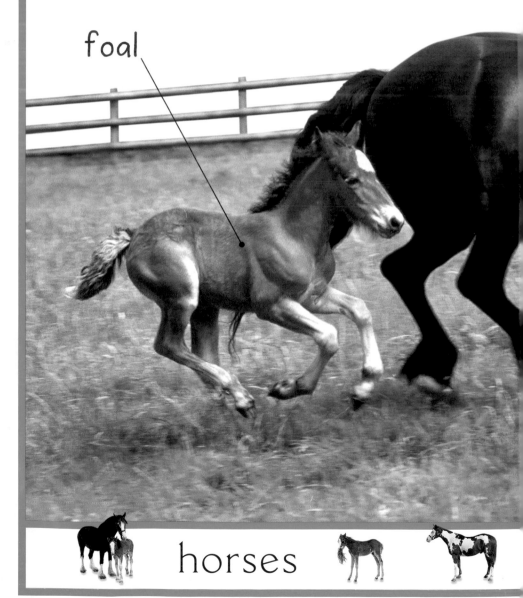

horses

mane

ponies

Here are two little ponies.

pony

Here is the cat
curled up with
her kitten.

kitten

 cats

hay

ear

Come see us again soon!

Moo!

Which animals

Neigh!

do you like best?

Picture word list

chicken

page 6

turkey

page 8

pig

page 10

cow

page 12

dog

page 14

sheep

page 16

goat

page 18

duck

page 20

goose

page 22

horse

page 24

pony

page 26

cat

page 28